Theos – clear thinking on religi

Theos is the UK's leading religion and society think tank. With our id combined circulation of 160 million in the past ten years, we are sha about the role of faith in contemporary society by means of high qua We provide a credible, informed and gracious Christian voice in our m

The Economist calls us "an organisation that demands attention", and Ju ⸻uggini, the influential atheist philosopher, has said "Theos provides rare proof that theology can be interesting and relevant even – perhaps especially – for those who do not believe."

To learn more, check us out on social media:

twitter.com/theosthinktank | facebook.com/theosthinktank | www.theosthinktank.co.uk

Why we exist

Religion has emerged as one of the key public issues of the 21st century, both nationally and globally. Our increasingly religiously-diverse society demands that we grapple with religion as a significant force in public life. Unfortunately, much of the debate about the role and place of religion has been unnecessarily emotive and ill-informed. We exist to change that.

We reject the notion of any possible 'neutral' perspective on these issues. We also reject the idea that religion is a purely private matter or that it is possible to divide public and private values for anyone.

We seek, rather, to recognise and analyse the ethical ideas and commitments that underlie public life and to engage in open and honest public debate, bringing the tradition of Christian social and political thought to bear on current issues. We believe that the mainstream Christian tradition has much to offer for a flourishing society.

What we do

Theos conducts research, publishes reports, and holds debates, seminars and lectures on the intersection of religion, politics and society in the contemporary world. We also provide regular comment for print and broadcast media and briefing and analysis to parliamentarians and policy makers. To date, Theos has produced over 50 research reports focusing on the big issues impacting British society, including welfare (*The Future of Welfare: A Theos Collection*), law (*"Speaking Up" – Defending and Delivering Access to Justice Today*), economics (*Just Money: How Catholic Social Teaching can Redeem Capitalism*), multiculturalism (*Making Multiculturalism Work*) and voting reform (*Counting on Reform*), as well as on a range of other religious, legal, political and social issues.

In addition to our independently-driven work, Theos provides research, analysis and advice to individuals and organisations across the private, public and not-for-profit sectors. Our staff and consultants have strong public affairs experience, an excellent research track record and a high level of theological literacy. We are practised in research, analysis, debate, and media relations.

Where we sit

We are committed to the traditional creeds of the Christian faith and draw on social and political thought from a wide range of theological traditions. We also work with many non-Christian and non-religious individuals and organisations.

Theos was launched with the support of the Archbishop of Canterbury and the Cardinal Archbishop of Westminster, but it is independent of any particular denomination. We are an ecumenical Christian organisation, committed to the belief that religion in general and Christianity in particular has much to offer for the common good of society as a whole. We are not aligned with any point on the party political spectrum, believing that Christian social and political thought cuts across these distinctions.

Join the discussion by becoming a Friend of Theos

Impact how society views Christianity and shape the cultural debate

The Friends' Programme is designed specifically for people who wish to enter the heart of the current debate. When you join, our commitment is to keep you informed, equipped, encouraged and inspired so that you can be a voice in the public square with us.

As a member of the Friends' Programme, you are provided with:

- *Hard copies of all our latest reports* on the most pressing issues – social justice, welfare, politics, spirituality, education, money, atheism, humanism…
- *Free access to our events.* Theos hosts a number of high calibre speakers (e.g. Rowan Williams, Larry Siedentop, Grace Davie) and debates ('Magna Carta and the future of liberty', 'Does humanism need Christianity?'). As a friend, you will receive invitations to all these without charge.
- *A network of like-minded people* who wish to share ideas and collaborate with one another. We host networking events which help you meet fellow Friends and build your own network, allowing ideas to flow and connections to form.
- *Our monthly e-newsletter* which is your one-stop digest for the latest news regarding religion and society.
- If you join as an Associate, you are *invited to private functions with the team*, allowing you to discuss upcoming projects, review the latest issues and trends in society, and have your say in where you see the public debate is going.

You can become a Friend or Associate today by visiting our website
www.theosthinktank.co.uk

If you'd prefer additional information, you can write to us directly:
Friends Programme, Theos, 77 Great Peter Street, London, SW1P 2EZ

If you have any inquiries regarding the Programme, you can email us at:
friends@theosthinktank.co.uk

That they all may be one:
Insights into Churches Together in England and contemporary ecumenism

Natan Mladin

Rachel Fidler

Ben Ryan

Published by Theos in 2017
© Theos
New Revised Standard Version Bible, copyright © 1989 the Division of Christian Education
of the National Council of the Churches of Christ in the United States of America. Used by
permission. All rights reserved.

ISBN 978-0-9956543-1-0

Theos
Licence Department
77 Great Peter Street
London
SW1P 2EZ

T 020 7828 7777
E hello@theosthinktank.co.uk
www.theosthinktank.co.uk

contents

acknowledgements

We would first like to thank the staff and board members of Churches Together in England who saw the need for this piece of work and trusted us to produce it. We hope this resource will help them plan wisely for the future of ecumenical work in England.

We are grateful for every Church representative and all other interviewees who generously gave up their time to share their thoughts on ecumenism and CTE. Without their input, this report would not have been possible.

As Research Director of Theos, Nick Spencer had general oversight of the project and offered us valuable insights and direction. Thanks, Nick! Imogen Ball was also very helpful in taking some of the interviews and putting together the graphs for the report. The other Theos team members who were not directly involved in the project were, as always, supportive and great fun to have around. Thanks, everyone!

Finally, we want to note just how encouraged we all were hearing the stories of Churches in England working together on mission and witness, showing and speaking the love of God in Christ.

preface

Unity is not optional. It is built into the very heart of being Christian, for in Christ we become citizens of his kingdom, members together of his body, bound together with all our brothers and sisters across the world. '…[Y]ou are', Peter said, 'a chosen race, a royal priesthood, a holy nation, God's own people, in order that you may proclaim the mighty acts of him who called you out of darkness into his marvellous light…' (1 Peter 2:9, NRSV). Mission and unity are therefore inseparable.

Churches Together in England was founded in 1990 to help the Churches in England explore how they could worship and witness together. During those 27 years the English Christian landscape has changed profoundly – that is reflected in CTE's growth from 16 members in 1990 to 44 today. There are many reasons for that: patterns of migration, new forms of spirituality, new ways of Christian discipleship. We are proud to represent that diversity, and eager to find ways in which we can work together in Christ's name as we respond to the needs and aspirations of our society.

We are grateful to Theos for its work in compiling this report. We hope that, with widespread study and discussion, it will help us grow closer to each other in our shared pathways of discipleship and in the mission we hold in common.

Archbishop Justin Welby
The Archbishop of Canterbury

Cardinal Vincent Nichols
The Cardinal Archbishop of Westminster

Revd Dr Hugh Osgood
The Free Churches Moderator

The Revd Canon Billy Kennedy
The President nominated by the New Churches, the Religious Society of Friends
(ie the Quakers) and the Lutheran and German-speaking Churches

Bishop Angaelos
The President for the Orthodox Churches

Bishop Dr Eric Brown
The Pentecostal President

executive summary

The **contemporary ecumenical landscape in England** is complex and continues to shift on account of the following factors:

- The general climate of church decline: a national trend of falling church attendance and Christian affiliation

- Economic and financial pressures faced by all Churches

- The huge diversity of Christian expression in the country

- The variety of views on Christian unity

- Differences regarding the specific focus of ecumenism

Important ecumenical progress has been made in the last twenty years. A significant number of Churches in England enjoy healthy relationships at the national level and collaborate vigorously at the local level.

Indeed, this research shows that today ecumenism is most vibrant at the local level. Local churches cross denominational boundaries and work together on different aspects of mission, most notably social action.

Correlated with this is a diminishing interest in pursuing the 'full visible unity' of the Church – one of the traditional aspirations of ecumenism. Our research revealed a strong emphasis on the need to appreciate differences between Churches as sources of mutual enrichment, and express practically the existing spiritual unity of the Church.

The good quality of relationships between Churches is due, in no small part, to the work done by **Churches Together in England (CTE)**, the country's main ecumenical instrument.

A majority of people interviewed and surveyed for this project highlighted the following strengths of CTE:

- CTE plays a vital role in developing and brokering relationships between Churches, particularly at the national level

- CTE provides a space for open conversations

- With 44 member Churches,[1] CTE reflects the diversity of Christianity in England

- CTE does its best work at the national level

- CTE is led and run in an exemplary way

Particular constituencies within CTE reported the following strengths:

- 'A place at the table': CTE membership offers validation and respectability particularly for smaller, newer or ethnic minority Churches or networks of churches

- CTE has the potential to amplify the voice of smaller Churches who wish to speak on issues which concern them

- CTE provides a number of practical benefits, including access to faith schools and chaplaincy

The following are **weaknesses or areas of concern in CTE** that came up across a broad range of interviews:

- Lack of clear vision and purpose: what is CTE for? What does it do uniquely? This was the fundamental weakness found to impinge on most aspects of its work

- Disproportionality in appeal to different Churches: larger Churches are less reliant on and expect less from CTE than newer, smaller Churches

- Lack of visibility and public profile

- Lack of clarity on funding: which members should fund (more)? How much? What are they in fact funding?

- Difficulties around 'speaking with one voice': on what issues? How can CTE best 'get the word out'?

- Some confusion about how Intermediate Bodies work and relate to CTE

- Relative absence of young people from ecumenism

Aside from these broadly shared concerns, there were a number of **specific areas of concern**, some of which have to do only with particular constituencies within CTE:

- A number of CTE member Churches do not divide themselves along national lines. This constrains their participation in ecumenism in important ways

- Some Churches are better placed than others to represent unified viewpoints in ecumenical conversations given variance in ecclesiology and organisational structures (some members hold to a more hierarchical and centralist ecclesiology, while others hold to a more decentralised and devolved ecclesiology)

- Orthodox and Catholic interviewees expressed concern about the predominance of a Protestant style of worship and Bible study in CTE meetings

- There is no common mind between liberal Protestant Churches and theologically conservative Churches on key ethical questions (e.g. human sexuality, gay marriage)

- Some members want CTE to broaden its agenda and engage more in inter-faith work

- The relationship with and participation of black and ethnic minority Churches remains a challenge, notwithstanding the important progress that has been made on this front

- The relationship between CTE and CTBI (Churches Together in Britain and Ireland) needs to be clarified

Possibilities for the future of ecumenism in England and recommendations for CTE:

Our research revealed a general desire for an ecumenism that is:

- Distinctly outward-orientated

- More firmly aligned with mission and witness

- Low-key, with nimble structures

- Attentive to and focused on the local level

- Fuelled by strong personal relationships

General recommendations for CTE:

1. Clarify and 'thicken' vision as a matter of urgency: all weaknesses and areas of concern correlate strongly with the absence of a clear vision

- Consider reshaping an ecumenical vision around mission

- Host substantive conversations on the nature, scope and practicalities of mission

2. Continue brokering new relationships and strengthening existing ones

3. Remain active at national level and consider ways in which to increase involvement at both national and international level

- 'Speak with one voice!': take on the challenge of discerning issues to speak on and the best processes to do so effectively

4. The public value of ecumenism: explore ways in which the disciplines and practices of ecumenism can be offered as a gift to the wider society (see point 3 above)

5. Consider being more intentional about becoming the primary facilitating, informing and enabling body for mission-focused ecumenical work in the country

Specific recommendations:

6. Gather information and success stories of ecumenical work at all levels, and disseminate widely and accessibly

7. Clarify relation to CTBI

8. Continue to find ways of drawing in the younger generation

executive summary – references

1   Number correct as of 16th August 2017.

introduction

This report seeks to offer an insight into contemporary ecumenism in England by evaluating the role played by Churches Together in England (CTE). Given its uniquely broad membership – with 44 member Churches,[2] covering a wide spectrum of Christian expression in England – and its strategic role in aiding and coordinating ecumenical efforts across the country, CTE makes for a compelling case study of English ecumenism. Beyond the particulars of CTE's strengths, weaknesses and areas of concern as an organisation, the report seeks to shed light on the contemporary ecumenical landscape in England. Its aim is to bring into focus key dynamics and challenges in the relationships between Churches in England, intimate something of the direction of travel of ecumenism in England, and suggest possibilities for the future.

Churches Together in England: a brief history

CTE is one of five 'ecumenical instruments' (or organisations) – along with Action of Churches Together in Scotland (ACTS), Churches Together in Wales (CYTÛN), the Irish Council of Churches (ICC), and the overarching Churches Together in Britain and Ireland (CTBI) – which were established in 1990 following the 1987 ecumenical conference in Swanwick. The Swanwick Conference was a watershed moment for British ecumenism. Among other things, it marked the transition from a 'Council of Churches' model, which had been dominant on the British ecumenical scene for more than 40 years, to the current 'Churches Together' model of ecumenism. This enabled the full participation of the Roman Catholic Church and greater participation from black-led Churches in British ecumenism.

The difference between the two can be explained briefly as follows. On the Council of Churches model, the Council would speak and act on behalf of member Churches. As a decision-making body it would make recommendations, seeking to drive the Churches' work towards visible Christian unity. The main problem with the model was that, despite the generally good quality of work produced and the successes in building relationships between Churches, the recommendations made by the Council were not always heeded, therefore exerting little influence on the life of the Churches themselves. The Council effectively operated as a separate structure alongside member Churches, to which it was not, however, accountable. With time, ecumenism came to be seen as an 'extra', a set of meetings and activities perceived to be only tenuously linked to the Churches' life and mission in the world.

Ecumenical instruments like CTE facilitate and aid inter-Church cooperation rather than seeking to implement a particular direction or agenda.

The 'Churches Together' model, on the other hand, rests on a 'bottom up' and 'grassroots' approach to ecumenism. Ecumenical instruments like CTE facilitate and aid inter-Church cooperation rather than seeking to implement a particular direction or agenda. Initiatives and partnerships between Churches have primacy and are meant to inform and shape the direction of ecumenical efforts at the national level through their respective 'national instrument'. The model is built on the principles of consultation and collaboration, which encourages the member Churches themselves to work together, share resources and discern the direction and strategy for expressing and strengthening Christian unity. Ecumenism, on this model, is not an extra set of priorities and activities for Churches to embrace, but "a dimension of all that [Churches] do which releases energy, through the sharing of resources".[3]

When it was first set up in 1990, CTE had 16 member Churches. Today the number of members has increased to 44. These are national denominations or networks of churches in England. Apart from the 44 members, a number of co-ordinating groups around various areas of interest, Bodies in Association (BiA)[4] and other Church agencies sit under the CTE umbrella. As an organisation CTE's declared aim is to help Churches in their efforts to see "a deepening of their communion with Christ and with one another in the Church, which is his body; and to fulfil their mission to proclaim the Gospel by common witness and service in the world."[5] CTE is served by a small team led by the General Secretary. The team works under the direction of the Board of Directors (Trustees) who are appointed by the 'Enabling Group', which brings together national representatives of the member Churches. CTE is represented by six presidents: The Archbishop of Canterbury; The Cardinal Archbishop of Westminster; The Free Churches Group Moderator; The President nominated by the New Churches, the Religious Society of Friends (i.e. the Quakers) and the Lutheran and German-speaking Churches; The President for the Orthodox Churches; and The Pentecostal President.

methodology

The research underpinning this report was conducted between September 2016 and June 2017. It has both a qualitative and a quantitative component. Most of the data were obtained through a total of 63 qualitative interviews, the majority of which were organised with representatives of CTE members. By 'data' we refer here mainly to perceptions, views, and evaluative comments on ecumenism generally, and CTE specifically, expressed by interviewees. These are synthesised and analysed below, and form the core of this report.

We also conducted a smaller number of interviews with individuals who, given their experience with, knowledge of, and previous or current responsibilities in some area of English ecumenical life, were recognised to have important insights.

The interviews with CTE's members were largely conducted with general secretaries (or equivalent roles), 'ecumenical officers' or other Church leaders with responsibilities for ecumenism. For the most part we organised one-on-one interviews. Where Church representatives requested it – given their particular ecclesial or organisational structure – we organised group interviews, where we spoke to two to six Church representatives.

> *Ecumenism is not an extra set of priorities and activities for Churches to embrace, but "a dimension of all that [Churches] do which releases energy, through the sharing of resources."*

We devised a structured discussion which covered key focus areas, including the reasons for ecumenical involvement of the member Churches, and the strengths of, limits of, and barriers to contemporary ecumenism. The guide also featured more questions related specifically to CTE and its role on the ecumenical scene. We generally concluded the interviews with questions around the future of ecumenism in England – asking interviewees to envisage the best and worst case scenarios, before suggesting ways in which CTE might play into that future. A list of all the interviews conducted as part of this research project is available in the Appendix to this report.

In addition to the 63 interviews conducted, we devised a written questionnaire which was circulated and filled in by a total of 44 respondents during CTE's Enabling Group meeting,[5] attended by representatives from each member Church, and CTE's National Pentecostal Forum,[6] both held in March 2017. The results of the questionnaire were helpful in the task of synthesising and structuring the data collected through the qualitative component of the research.

structure

This report consists of four main parts. In this first part we offer a brief theological discussion of ecumenism. We home in on two key concepts within ecumenical theology – unity and mission. We connect these to the findings of our research, outlining different visions of unity and ecumenism that we came across. We go on to present some of the features of the ecumenical scene in England and reflect on some of the general challenges of the present context.

The second part of the report is a distillation of the views of CTE members on the strengths and successes of CTE and contemporary ecumenism in England. This is followed, by a section which examines the weaknesses and areas of concern. Both parts distinguish between strengths and weaknesses identified by a significant number of interviewees, and specific strengths and weaknesses which were mentioned by a smaller number or a sub-set of interviewees. The report concludes with some evaluative comments and outlines a series of possibilities for moving into the future. We begin with a few theological comments about ecumenism and its foundational concept: unity.

introduction – references

1   In keeping with CTE's practice, in this report we use the capitalised form 'Church/es' in an inclusive way, conscious that no generic term exists to perfectly fit the variety of ecclesial self-understanding and self-description of CTE members (e.g. denomination, fellowship, union, federation). For clarity purposes, in contexts where the use of the word 'Church' might confusingly suggest a 'local church' rather than the denomination, we have chosen to use the term 'denomination' (e.g. 'the leader of a large Pentecostal denomination').

2   Colin Davey, *Parish Priorities: Ecumenism*, (BCC/CTS, 1988).

3   'Bodies in Association' are interdenominational associations of Christians working together for a particular purpose (e.g. Action for Children, Bible Society, Church Action on Poverty)

4   http://www.cte.org.uk/Groups/234695/Home/About/Basis_of_CTE/Basis_of_CTE.aspx. Site accessed 25 July 2017.

5   *The Enabling Group* (EG) is the principal meeting for CTE members. It is attended by representatives from each member Church, Intermediate Bodies (discussed further down in the report), and other Christian organisations associated with CTE.

6   *National Pentecostal Forum* is a bi-annual meeting that brings together representatives of twenty national CTE members that belong to the Pentecostal and charismatic traditions.

1

ecumenism and the question of unity

Traditionally at the heart of ecumenism lies the issue of Church unity. Ecumenism begins with the recognition that the Church is conspicuously divided and fragmented. This is an uncontested fact that needs little explanation. Theologically, however, ecumenism begins

> *Ecumenism is the effort to express the spiritual unity of the Church and the pursuit of the Church's greater 'visible unity', so 'that the world may believe'.*

from the fact that the Church is indivisibly 'one, holy, catholic and apostolic'.[1] Ecumenism stretches between these two conflicting facts, one sociological and the other theological. It is, on the one hand, the effort to express the Church's unity and wholeness which are rooted in the Tri-unity of God and God's redemptive work in the world. Yet ecumenism is also the pursuit of the Church's greater 'visible unity' so 'that the world may believe' (Jn. 17:21, NRSV).

Another way of putting this is to say that, theologically, unity has two dimensions: gift and calling. Unity is, firstly, a gift. It is given in the very makeup of the Church as the One Body of Christ ("There is one body and one Spirit, just as you were called to one hope when you were called; one Lord, one faith, one baptism; one God and Father of all, who is over all and through all and in all." Eph. 4:4-6, NRSV).

This is the Church's fundamental, spiritual unity. The so-called High Priestly prayer of Jesus for the unity of His followers, recorded in John 17, has, in a crucial sense, been answered in the very constitution of the Church through the pouring of the Spirit. This enduring, spiritual unity is realised and maintained by the Spirit of Christ ("Make every effort to keep the *unity of the Spirit* through the bond of peace." Eph. 4:3, NRSV, emphasis added).

Yet this gift of spiritual unity is to be publicly expressed. It is to be lived out and shared with the world, "that the world may believe" (Jn. 17:21, NRSV) and people from every tongue, nation and culture be drawn into God's Kingdom of light, love, and life. This imperative to express the given spiritual unity, as witness to the world, is intimately related to the 'calling' dimension of unity. On this view, unity is also a *calling* that the Church, in all of its diversity and with all of its differences, is mandated to pursue in order to live out its missional nature faithfully, sent into the world as the Father sent the Son (Jn. 20:21, NRSV).

features of the English ecumenical landscape

So far we have looked at ecumenism and the question of unity in theological terms. In the following section, we move to look at the current reality, and seek to shed light on the ecumenical landscape in England and CTE.

To say that the picture of contemporary ecumenism in England is complicated is to say very little. It is, nonetheless, to say something true. This is largely explained by the significant changes in the landscape of Christianity in the UK.

While the number of people who call themselves Christian has sharply declined in the last decades, Christianity has become increasingly diverse, with a host of independent, migrant and ethnic minority Churches, mainly from the Pentecostal-Charismatic tradition, springing up and experiencing growth. There is also a wealth of inter-denominational and non-denominational organisations, agencies, and initiatives which are effectively ecumenical. They fulfil some of the traditional aims of ecumenical efforts (e.g. cooperation between different factions of Christianity on specific causes and initiatives), but do not self-identify as ecumenical and, importantly, operate outside traditional ecumenical structures (e.g. ecumenical instruments and their wider networks).

> *To say that the picture of contemporary ecumenism in England is complicated is to say very little. It is, nonetheless, to say something true. This is largely explained by the significant changes in the landscape of Christianity in the UK.*

 On a broader level, it is fair to say that the traditional models of ecumenism, with top-down structures, and formal dialogues between professionals within hard denominational structures has increasingly given way to a more relational, action-orientated and grass-roots form of ecumenism. In the evangelical Protestant world but, importantly for CTE, not in the Catholic or Orthodox worlds, this is coupled with a softening of denominational boundaries.

All of this, in the context of a growing diversity of Christian expression in England makes for an untidy yet vibrant 'ecumenical scene'. The section below looks in greater detail at this scene, focusing on the different views of unity and ecumenism among CTE members.

visions of unity and ecumenism among CTE members

The two dimensions of the Church's unity – as *gift* to be celebrated and expressed, and as *calling* to be pursued – belong to the core of Christian teaching. It is important to note that acknowledging the existing spiritual unity of the Church does not preclude the *calling* to preserve, deepen, and express it publicly. Indeed, the gift and calling dimensions of unity must not be separated or pitted against each other.

Still, our research revealed that the majority of CTE members place greater emphasis on the 'gift' dimension of unity. We heard numerous comments to the effect that unity in Christ is something to be celebrated and expressed practically through collaboration on various aspects of Christian mission and witness. This chimes with what we discovered is a growing appetite for and involvement in practical ecumenism or, as Archbishop Justin Welby calls it, an "ecumenism of action" (see 'Inter-Church cooperation at local level' in the graph below), found to be particularly vibrant at the local level.

 As a point of contrast, a sizeable number of interviews revealed a general weariness with the ecumenism of previous decades, particularly its formal aspect, which was perceived to be, as one interviewee put it, "hugely lacking in energy". Indeed, it is fair to say those who placed more emphasis on the 'calling' aspect of unity, seeing unity as something to be worked towards and realised, were fewer and seemed resigned to the fact that "reaching visible unity" had turned out to be an elusive ideal. Having said that, it is worth noting at this point the growing popularity of the concept and methods of 'receptive ecumenism', particularly but not exclusively among those concerned with the 'calling' dimension of ecumenism.

Reception, according to David Nelson and Charles Raith II, is "one of the most significant concepts for understanding the history and theology of modern ecumenism".[2] The concept goes back to Cardinal Kasper, President Emeritus of the Pontifical Council for Promoting Christian Unity, while the methodology owes most to Paul Murray, the Professor of Catholic Studies at Durham University.[3] The essence of receptive ecumenism can be encapsulated in the following questions, which Churches are encouraged to ask themselves: 'what can we learn from each other as Churches?' 'what gifts must we receive from others, recognising that we do not possess everything we need to be faithful, fruitful and fully ourselves?'

Receptive ecumenism, as its advocates stress, is not about diluting or abandoning particular ecclesial identities, but about mutual enrichment, hospitality, listening, and gift exchange:[4] 'receiving Christ in the other'.[5] Since 2006 there have been several international conferences on receptive ecumenism. Paul Murray and the Durham Centre for Catholic Studies continue to develop projects to explore the practical outworking of the concept. CTE has also created resources for local use.[6] Our research revealed a general awareness of and, in some cases, a clear commitment to the principles of receptive ecumenism.

As previously noted, however, the majority of interviewees thought of ecumenism and unity in terms of cooperation, with Churches 'working together' on social action at community level. These were keen to note that what has been declining is commitment to a particular institutional-structural understanding of unity and the traditional means for pursuing it. What remains fairly healthy, as the graph below makes clear, is a commitment to a unity that is demonstrated through cooperation between Churches at the local level. The vast majority of Church leaders gave examples of ecumenical partnerships on social action, highlighting personal relationships between leaders as key to this end. More comments on this are to be found in the section on 'Specific weaknesses' and the concluding section on 'Possibilities for the future'.

The majority of interviewees thought of ecumenism and unity in terms of cooperation, with Churches 'working together' on social action at community level.

Which vision of ecumenism do you resonate with most?

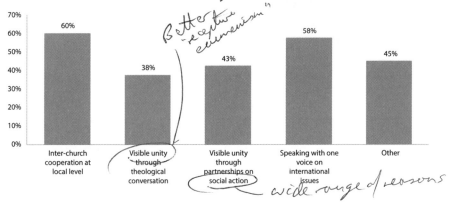

Though we found consensus on the relationship between unity and mission (the two fundamental notions of ecumenism), our research revealed no single understanding of what should be the focus of ecumenism. The graph above captures something of the messiness of contemporary conversations about ecumenism. In the questionnaire we devised, representatives of CTE members were asked to select one or more visions of ecumenism with which they resonated. The choices they were offered were gleaned primarily from the interviews we had conducted up to that point. Sixty per cent of those surveyed identified working together at the local level – most often on social action projects such as food banks, street pastors and homelessness interventions – as the view they resonated with most.

The second most popular vision of ecumenism among our questionnaire respondents was 'speaking with one voice' on international issues, such as the persecution of Christians and human trafficking. Indeed, the interviews we conducted throughout the research period revealed a more general appetite for speaking with one voice, primarily but not exclusively through the presidents of CTE. The opportunity and challenge this presents for CTE is briefly discussed in the final section of the report.

Most of the respondents to our questionnaire who selected 'other' indicated that they resonated with all the visions put forward and suggested these should not be split apart but seen as complimentary aspects of a 'rounded ecumenism'.

the mission of the Church within the missio Dei

The majority of interviewees who gravitated towards the 'gift' dimension of unity and who emphasised collaboration, almost invariably brought up the topics of witness and mission. Indeed, one of the recurrent themes in the 63 interviews conducted was, unsurprisingly, mission. "Unity is one side of the ecumenical coin, mission is the other", one interviewee said, stressing that the two should not be separated in thinking about and engaging in ecumenism.

> *The mission of God, to redeem, reconcile and renew the world, establishes and frames the mission of the Church.*

Those who brought up mission referred to it as being not simply a set of activities or practical initiatives that the Church engages in, but rather an active and multidimensional participation in the *missio Dei* (the mission of God). On this view, the mission of God, to redeem, reconcile and renew the world, establishes and frames the mission of the Church. Importantly, the Church's mission consists of, but is not restricted to evangelisation. It includes discipleship, social action, the pursuit of justice, and care for creation.

But beware less of "salvation"

This holistic and theologically grounded view of mission received a clear articulation at the 1952 International Missionary Conference in Willingen, Germany. Since then it has slowly filtered through the work of ecumenical bodies and denominations across the globe. The findings of our research bear this out. Many interviewees displayed an awareness of this expansive and holistic understanding of mission and wanted CTE to be even more intentionally mission-orientated than has so far been the case.

chapter 1 – references

1   These four distinctive adjectives describe the so-called 'Four Marks of the Church' which appear in the Niceo-Constantinopolitan Creed of 381, one of the foundational creeds of the Christian faith: "[I believe] in one, holy, catholic, and apostolic Church."

2   R. David Nelson & Charles Raith II, *Ecumenism. A Guide for the Perplexed* (London: Bloomsbury T&T Clark, 2017), 123.

3   See Paul D. Murray (ed.), *Receptive Ecumenism and the Call to Catholic Learning: Exploring a Way for Contemporary Ecumenism* (New York: Oxford University Press, 2008).

4   Peter Leithart, 'Receptive ecumenism' in *First Things*, 27 February 2015, https://www.firstthings.com/web-exclusives/2015/02/receptive-ecumenism. Site accessed 17 August 2017.

5   Personal correspondence with David Cornick.

6   See http://www.cte.org.uk/Groups/91312/Home/Resources/Theology/Receptive_Ecumenism/What_is_Receptive/What_is_Receptive.aspx. Site accessed 17 August 2017.

CTE's strengths

The section above set out some of the theoretical issues around ecumenism in general, touching on how these wider questions impact the specific focuses of ecumenism today. In this (and the following) section we look at the work of CTE as a key ecumenical instrument in England, identifying, on the basis of interviews with member Churches and key external voices, its main strengths and weaknesses.

As mentioned earlier on, unlike older conciliar models of ecumenism, CTE operates as a 'facilitative' membership organisation. This throws up an initial difficulty when trying to pinpoint the strengths of CTE as an ecumenical body – primarily because its capacity to achieve success, however defined, depends largely on the activity of its members and representatives. A number of interviewees voiced their particular discomfort when asked what they "get out" of CTE (i.e. how it specifically benefits them), for example. As one interviewee put it, CTE exists to "encourage, enable, prompt, and challenge the Churches themselves to engage ecumenically at every level." In this sense, interviewees generally believed that the benefits of CTE membership should and will always be proportionate to the effort that each Church "puts in."

> CTE exists to "encourage, enable, prompt, and challenge the Churches themselves to engage ecumenically at every level."

There are benefits that some Churches receive as a result of membership, which do not imply wider ecumenical success per se. For example, for parents from smaller Churches, membership of CTE provides a level of 'legitimacy' which enables their children to attend faith schools. Whilst an obvious benefit of membership, practical 'perks' like this were not always spoken about with any overtly ecumenical emphasis. This makes the identification of CTE's 'strengths' more complex than may be initially expected. Whilst the majority interviewed were quick to voice strengths of CTE, one member warned: "CTE should keep in mind that the fruit of its work is not always measurable, which I know can be hard when you're reviewing something."

Nevertheless, there was significant consensus across those interviewed and surveyed that membership provides a number of obvious and identifiable benefits. These named 'general' strengths are aspects that the majority of CTE's member Churches and staff appreciated about CTE. There were also strengths common to particular groups of members within CTE, which though not representative across the board, were still important to certain constituencies. These will be called 'particular' strengths, and will be returned to in the next section.

general strengths

Those strengths that were commonly recognised across a wide range of interviews were:

1   Broker of relationships

   i   Strengthening unity

   ii   The Enabling Group:[1] relationships between national representatives

   iii   The Forum[2]

2   Conversations

3   Scope and diversity

   i   Diversity in practice

   ii   'Richness' of variety

4   National level activity

5   Leadership and staff

1   "broker of relationships"

The most frequently mentioned 'general' strength of CTE, voiced repeatedly across the entire range of membership, is the role it plays in developing and maintaining relationships – between both individuals and Churches. The majority of interviewees valued the personal connections with fellow Church leaders formed through CTE as well as more formal Church-to-Church relationships.

In our questionnaire we asked the following question about the function of CTE: "If CTE could only do one of the following things, what should it be?" Options included theological resourcing and training; brokering and developing relationships; promoting inter-faith dialogue; developing social justice projects, and advocacy on national and international issues. An overall majority (61%) of respondents expressed their desire for CTE to broker and develop relationships over and against all other emphases. Second most common was advocacy on national and international issues down at 11%, showing just how much of a priority relationships are to member Churches compared with other areas of activity.

If CTE could only do one of the following things, what should that be?

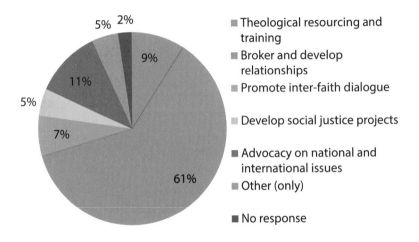

5% 2%

9%

11%

5%

7%

61%

- Theological resourcing and training
- Broker and develop relationships
- Promote inter-faith dialogue

- Develop social justice projects

- Advocacy on national and international issues
- Other (only)

- No response

CTE's important role in building these relationships came up repeatedly in face-to-face interviews, with members generally naming it CTE's biggest success to date. The leader of a large Church said that the "main success" of CTE is simply that "it gathers". He pointed out CTE's invaluable and unique role in this, claiming: "that's what it uniquely does and has done well. At both a national and local level, it would be tragic to lose this gathering role."

CTE's important role in building these relationships came up repeatedly in face-to-face interviews. The "main success" of CTE is simply that "it gathers".

"The best thing that CTE does at the minute," said another interviewee, who attends the Enabling Group, "is it allows for friendships to happen." This interviewee recognised the important role CTE plays in developing relationships at a variety of levels, both on a national level and in "fostering and nurturing local ecumenical work and partnerships."

This view was not limited to larger, older Churches, but was expressed across the entire spectrum of membership. When asked what CTE does best at the moment, for example, a Church leader from a newer, Pentecostal Church replied: "It has facilitated good Church connections throughout the country." Another key figure from a smaller charismatic Church said CTE's main success is: "bringing people together and creating relationships."

i relationships strengthening unity

Interviewees' strong appreciation for relationships formed through CTE was often bound up with claims about the nature of Christian unity and the wider goal of ecumenism. There was a shared appreciation for the absolute centrality of relationships to achieving unity, however defined.

An interviewee from a large Church said that the "end goal" of ecumenism is to reflect the "theological truth that we are one," for which "you need person-to-person but also Church-to-Church relationships." One representative of another Church claimed: "What gift can Christians give to the world if not better relations? It's central to everything. ... No model of ecumenism works unless the personal is there." These statements symbolise the wider shift away from a unity that needs to be 'realised', to a given unity that has to be practically expressed.

> "What gift can Christians give to the world if not better relations? It's central to everything." We "become more ourselves when we learn from one another".

There was a shared appreciation for inter-Church relationships as furthering the flourishing of each separate Church. "What really brings out the best of any group," one leader of a Pentecostal Church remarked, "is when genuine relationships are built." We "become more ourselves when we learn from one another," another interviewee commented.

ii relationships between national representatives and leaders

On the whole, the relationships developed between Church leaders at a national level were considered particularly successful. Whilst relationships at the intermediate (operating at regional level)[3] and local levels were valuable to some interviewees, comments on these areas were less frequent. Of course it is hard to say to what extent CTE's national level relationships impact relationships at the other two levels, but vibrant relationships at these lower levels were not necessarily associated with CTE directly. This is explored in more detail at the end of this chapter.

The strength of relationships between national Church representatives was commented upon across the board. When asked whether CTE offers anything different to other ecumenical bodies, an interviewee from an older Church responded that it provides access to fellow leaders from a uniquely broad spectrum of Churches. A Pentecostal leader remarked that CTE "brings together the presidents in a very successful way," so it now becomes "second nature to those in those roles to want to work together." Another interviewee commented that the presidents' meetings act as a "catalyst for relationships," of which "Archbishop Justin [Welby] has been quite key."

iii   The Forum

Beyond the strength of relationships formed between leaders at the national level, there was a shared appreciation for certain 'spaces' within CTE as relational catalysts for Church representatives more broadly. There was praise across the board for the role of the Forum in gathering people from a broad spectrum of Churches. The Forum is a non-decision-making gathering organised by CTE every three years. It brings together over 300 representatives of CTE's member Churches, regional ecumenical bodies, ecumenical interest groups and other interdenominational organisations. It is the largest representative gathering of the Churches in England.

One CTE member of staff remarked that the Forum "offers opportunity for people to come together from a large number of constituencies across the whole of England" and "gives the context for a number of people to share together". "I'm not sure you get that anywhere else," she commented. A representative of a relatively small Church commented that "at the minute it [the Forum] creates a safe space for Church leaders and representatives to come and work together where we can." A number of interviewees referred to it as a "safe space," where relationships are formed in a genuine, open and honest context.

There was widespread agreement that the Forum successfully gathers groups of Churches that may otherwise never interact. One Orthodox interviewee commented that the biggest advantage they see from membership of CTE, for example, is meeting with other Orthodox members at the Forum that they're not in formal communion with.

2   conversations

Closely linked to the role of the Forum as a 'space' for building relationships, is CTE's role in facilitating honest and open conversations. One leader of a large Church, for example, claimed that he "doesn't think CTE should be a place people fear the conversation," believing this to be "one of its valuable offerings." A significantly smaller Church with more recent CTE membership claimed CTE provides "a useful structure through which to have discussions." Another comparatively small Church said they value the formal and informal contexts to "ask questions" within CTE, appreciating the "conversations that take place in the Enabling Group."

Though views were mixed on the content of these conversations, some kind of space for general honest and open dialogue was believed to be valuable by the majority of interviewees. CTE's provision of "safe spaces" like the Enabling Group and the Forum were generally seen as necessary for this.

3 scope and diversity – bringing together such a variety of Churches

Praise for CTE's diversity of membership and 'welcoming' spirit also came up repeatedly, voiced across a range of Churches. Its broad scope was felt to be both unique and invaluable, and was generally listed as one of its main strengths.

Partially with regard to the variety of CTE membership, we asked respondents to the questionnaire for their opinion on the following comment made by one interviewee: "CTE has become too diffuse for its own good". Fifty-four per cent of respondents either disagreed or strongly disagreed with the statement, with 12% agreeing (32% expressing ambivalence and 2% not responding).

'CTE has become too diffuse for its own good'

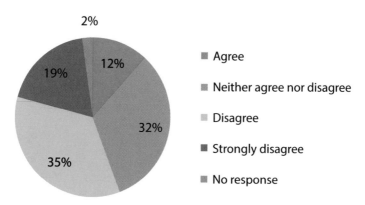

More active appreciation for CTE's diversity came out in the interviews. One president of a large Church claimed CTE's biggest success is that it is "probably the only grouping that gathers such a broad spectrum" of Churches. A leader within a large Church with a long history of ecumenical engagement in England also claimed that CTE is the "only place nationally bringing this number of Churches together." When asked whether CTE's expansion is a "good thing," a Church leader replied that it is a "huge opportunity for the members" in terms of "working together and building relationships."

There was also appreciation for CTE embracing and reflecting the current diverse landscape of Christianity in England. "This is the reality" the above leader continued, "and we need to respond to it." Though not without difficulties (equal representation, the challenge of categorisation, diversity of visions, and the issue of finding a shared language), the shift was seen by the majority of historic Churches as an overall positive. Indeed, the interviews we conducted revealed that the majority of members value CTE's growth in membership.

It is worth noting that the 32% who 'neither agree[d] nor disagree[d]' with the statement that 'CTE has become too diffuse for its own good', and the 12% who agreed with it, point to a fundamental difficulty inherent in an umbrella organisation of such breadth and diversity as CTE. We will look at this in greater detail in the 'weaknesses' section below.

On the further expansion of CTE, we asked respondents to react to the following statement: 'CTE should actively seek to grow in number'. Fifty per cent responded positively to the statement, with just 9% disagreeing (the remaining 41% selected 'neither agree nor disagree'). Whilst only around half positively encouraged growth, therefore, few members were actively against it. It should also be pointed out that some respondents did not reply to this statement enthusiastically for want of a more 'organic' kind of growth. This view was expressed in the comments section that followed the survey question. This was indicated in the comments section following the survey question. Yet the way in which CTE's expanding membership works out in practice deserves separate attention.

i   diversity in practice

Notwithstanding the challenges of a broad membership, the majority of interviewees were complimentary about the way diversity is handled in practice. One national representative from an Orthodox Church admired the fact that despite the "range of theologies and cultures among 44 member Churches," he has "never heard or seen clashes." "Everyone respects everybody and does their best to work together. There are conversations, discussions and debate but not conflict," a Church leader remarked. A CTE member of staff commented on the Forum as a place where diversity is valued, respected and maintained. It is "not limited to a particular theology," the person noted.

"It's genuinely open, with a huge breadth of theology and churchmanship." Freedom of Churches to worship in different ways and to keep their distinctiveness was generally seen as a main strength of CTE.

ii 'richness' of variety

Most of the interviewees who expressed appreciation for CTE's growing membership also placed great emphasis on the 'gift' dimension of unity discussed in the first section of this report. "The essence of fellowship is meeting with people who are ethnically, culturally and theologically different," an interviewee remarked. Another representative for a historic Church expressed

> "The essence of fellowship is meeting with people who are ethnically, culturally and theologically different."

enthusiasm for the "rich variety of experience and insight throughout the Church and the world" and said that to "lose all that by bringing it into one homogenous whole would be a shame." "We are all part of the body of Christ," he said, "as long as we share basic Trinitarian beliefs." A key leader of another Church reinforced the above, claiming the "main purpose" of ecumenism is to "exist alongside other Churches freely worshipping in different ways."

There were others who, while also appreciating CTE's increasing membership base, still believed denominational differences were ultimately something to be overcome in this life. In doing so, it is fair to say they were emphasising the 'calling' aspect of unity. There was, however, general agreement that a unity achieved through the collapsing, or even downplaying, of denominational differences would be a decidedly unwelcome prospect.

4   national level activity

The second most common response to the survey question "If CTE could only do one of the following things, what should it be?" was advocacy on national and international issues. This came up repeatedly across interviews; with many believing CTE's strongest current work takes place at a national level. Appreciation for CTE's national level activity was generally commented upon by people working at the highest level, as well as many representatives from small and minority Churches (which we will return to in more depth in the 'particular' strengths section).

One CTE president remarked, for example, that CTE "carries weight nationally," which gives it "the potential to have huge influence." "The national is where CTE seems to be positioned best," he continued, believing Archbishop Justin Welby's media profile to be uniquely influential. A member of CTE staff said CTE's strongest work at the moment is "picking up on national issues and the ways the Church can support them" (e.g. human trafficking). He claimed, "CTE's role is behind the scenes and national, fanning the flames of the transformative work that goes on amongst communities." He claimed initiatives like "Thy Kingdom Come" are the "future" of CTE. His appreciation for CTE's national engagement was reflected in his vision of ecumenism more generally, as a mission for the "whole inhabited earth."

Appreciation for CTE's work on a national level was understandably valued by interviewees from smaller, ethnic/cultural minority Churches at a variety of levels, as well as by the national leaders mentioned above. When asked what CTE does best, the leader of a Pentecostal denomination replied, "CTE has the standing to speak for the Church, so if CTE says something, it's meaty." He believes that CTE has a good standing amongst those outside of the Church, making it well positioned for national advocacy. Another Pentecostal Church leader claimed one of the best things he gets out of CTE is being "invited to meetings on national issues like the refugee crisis," where he can get his voice heard.

> CTE "carries weight nationally," which gives it "the potential to have huge influence."

5   leadership and staff

Another general strength which repeatedly came up was the leadership style of General Secretary Rev Dr David Cornick. A significant number of interviewees brought this up largely unprompted. He "isn't pushy" one member remarked. "You can put the six presidents in a room and he doesn't dominate, which is true of the way he runs the whole of CTE." Another leader of a large Church claimed "for David, it's grassroots up…his view is to let our member Churches determine our shape."

"I've got the highest praise for David Cornick," one leader said. "He is a remarkable man. His insight into ecumenism is something I value very much. He always brings something important to the table." He is "a good leader and he's fair," said another interviewee, expressing a common concern about the difficulty of finding a suitable leader to take his place.

The helpfulness of the rest of the CTE staff was also highlighted frequently during the interviews. Several leaders made positive comments about the efficient way in which the office was run, despite scarcity of resources and relatively few people on staff.

particular strengths

Beyond these general strengths recognised across the spectrum of CTE's membership, there were also benefits that came up repeatedly in particular constituencies within CTE. Though not representative of all Churches, these strengths were nevertheless seen as resoundingly important to certain cohorts.

1 "a place at the table"

Linked to CTE's national presence and activity, a particular section of members expressed appreciation for CTE's "kudos". This included newer Churches, smaller Churches, ethnic and cultural minority Churches, and those with less history of ecumenical engagement. CTE with its national weight was generally considered a "validating mechanism" for many within this constituency, which we have already briefly touched upon.

> *CTE with its national weight was generally considered a "validating mechanism".*

A benefit repeatedly voiced across this constituency was the feeling of being "part of the national picture," as one national representative commented, which for "relatively small groups" is "really important." When asked about the main thing that his denomination gets out of CTE, for example, the leader of one older Pentecostal denomination replied, "It gives credibility from the outside-in, when agencies outside of the Church see we are connected to the recognised state Church [sic]… In the minds of certain public agencies it carries certain kudos to be part of it." Another Pentecostal representative similarly said that one of their main motivations for joining CTE was to gain "respectability and be a part of the British Church." "We feel part of the national Church," he continued, "so we want to be part of the national ecumenical instrument."

It is also important to point out that joining a body with "kudos" was not seen as wholly positive by Churches that didn't have a lot of previous engagement in ecumenism. One national representative expressed concern that people mistakenly see it largely as an Anglican project in which other Churches are simply seen as collaborating with the state Church. This was something that was voiced several times by smaller, ethnic/cultural minority Churches (including several black majority Pentecostal denominations, and Orthodox Churches).

2 practical benefits of CTE membership

The weight CTE carries amongst public agencies ensures certain practical benefits for members. Though not true of every Church and individual interviewed, the balance of opinion amongst newer Churches, smaller Churches, ethnic or cultural minority Churches, and those with little history of ecumenical engagement was that these practical benefits were a key motivator for joining CTE. The same Pentecostal leader who spoke of his denomination being given "credibility" through CTE claimed that a "huge benefit" of membership is that children from member Churches are eligible for entry into faith schools. A national representative mentioned being "nudged into CTE through chaplaincy," as the job can often require the denomination to be a member.[4] It is true that membership of a Church that is a member of CTE generally helps those seeking a chaplaincy post.

A leader from a large Pentecostal denomination commented on the practical benefits beyond chaplaincy, ease of admission to faith schools and attendance of 'state events'. "Beyond engagement in public life, he continued, there is the other practical benefit of common resources. [Through] together joining resources, we can achieve things that [my Church] and other Churches couldn't do on their own."

3 amplifying "voice"

The Archbishop of Canterbury "get headline"

> CTE also gives smaller Churches a means of actually joining in and shaping the conversation.

Beyond providing practical benefits, the majority of Orthodox, Pentecostal, ethnic minority, and smaller Churches saw CTE as a means of getting their voice amplified. Beyond the "kudos" and practical benefits of CTE, it also gives these Churches a means of actually joining in and shaping the conversation. Having "a place at the table," is for a lot of these Churches seen as platform to speak into and influence the current climate.

A leader of an older Pentecostal denomination commented, we "get invited into the conversation when there are issues which affect our communities… When looking for a voice they will look for a Church that is respectable and can speak for a cross-section of the Church, rather than an independent pastor." A Lutheran representative was appreciative that CTE "provides a forum for us to express our voice and to join in." He claimed that their voice is particularly "magnified" through CTE's media presence and national representatives. Interviewees did not generally want to have their voice amplified for the sake of it, but because they felt they could make a "valuable contribution," which "enriches the ecumenical scene."

Views on the equal representation of voices within CTE were mixed amongst the smaller Churches. Whilst some within this constituency believed their voices were under-represented, one Church leader remarked, "the Church of England and the Roman Catholics are big players in CTE, but I'm grateful that they don't have any more representation than us."

conclusion

As we can see, CTE has a number of successful aspects that are seen as both identifiable and invaluable to its members. The important role it plays in facilitating relationships and incorporating a wide range of Churches is seen as particularly significant. These should be encouragements that CTE is fulfilling a valuable role in English Church life.

There were a number of other strengths voiced by some interviewees that haven't been included in this report, simply because it would be misleading to present them as representative. One strength that was mentioned by a few interviewees was the role CTE plays in resourcing, for example, in the training and support of ecumenical officers, the general support of staff, providing resources for local ecumenical partnerships, and circulating information. This is clearly significant, but only a few of the interviewees brought it up.

Another area that was valued by a majority of members was CTE's role in local level ecumenism. The survey results showed 59% of respondents either disagreeing or strongly disagreeing with the claim "CTE is not needed for local ecumenical partnerships". Several interviewees highlighted that relationships at the national level, where CTE plays a significant role, is an important factor that enables collaboration between Churches at the local level.

The next section examines, first, some of the general weaknesses and areas of concern with regards to CTE and, second, zeroes in on weaknesses perceived as such by certain constituencies within CTE's membership (described in this report as 'specific weaknesses').

chapter 2 – references

1   The 'Enabling Group' is the meeting of CTE's members and has the task of nurturing ecumenism in England. It considers matters of governance and common concern. The Enabling Group is the place where the trustees of CTE report to Member Churches and are offered direction for the future.

2   The 'Forum' is a non-deliberative gathering organised by CTE every three years. It brings together over 300 representatives of CTE's Member Churches, Intermediate (ecumenical) Bodies, Co-ordinating Groups and Bodies in Association. It is the largest representative gathering of the Churches in England. For more information, visit http://www.cte.org.uk/ Groups/279029/Home/About/CTE_Governance/The_Forum/What_is_the.aspx

3   Intermediate level ecumenism is discussed in the next chapter, under 'general weaknesses and areas of concern'.

4   Some chaplaincies, particularly in prisons and healthcare, require a chaplain to be part of a registered denomination or group. A Church which is part of CTE is able to put that on applications forms for chaplaincy to demonstrate their legitimacy. In some cases that is a necessity, in others, merely helpful.

CTE's weaknesses and areas of concern

The section above looked at the strengths of CTE as an ecumenical body. In the same way this section draws on the evidence from interviews and surveys to analyse those aspects of CTE which were perceived as weaknesses or challenges for the organisation. Just as with the section on strengths above these have been divided between those which were 'general' (i.e. were commonly recognised across a broad range of interviews) and those which were more specific (identified by only a smaller sub-section of interviewees, usually from within a particular constituency).

general weaknesses and areas of concern

Those weaknesses and areas of concern which were commonly recognised across a wide range of interviews were:

1   A thin vision

2   Disproportionality in appeal to different Churches & weight vs size

3   Lack of public profile

4   Finance

5   Lack of nimbleness

6   Intermediate Bodies (IBs)

7   Lack of appeal to the next generation

8   Church decline

Not all of these were named by all interviewees, and some were of greater concern to some groups than others, but these eight areas and topics arose consistently across a range of interviews and (unlike some of the specific weaknesses discussed later) were not unique to any particular constituency or theological tradition.

1   a thin vision

> *It is difficult to clearly articulate the vision and purpose of CTE as an organisation. The diversity of CTE membership entails the absence of a single dominant vision of unity and ecumenism.*

What is CTE fundamentally for? There are a number of potential answers to that question, as has been made clear in other parts of this report. However, as one interviewee put it "there is a missing strapline". That is not literally true, the strapline is "a visible sign... deepening communion... sharing the Gospel together... making connections", but it does point to a factor identified by a large number of interviewees, that it is difficult to clearly articulate the vision and purpose of CTE as an organisation. It is worth stressing that this may, to some extent, mirror a broader sense of uncertainty as to the purpose of ecumenism in general. The diversity of CTE membership entails the absence of a single dominant vision of unity and ecumenism.

A point made by some interviewees, particularly those who had had a long involvement in ecumenical activities is that to some extent the excitement and sense of purpose around ecumenism has faded. This is partly because, as several interviewees put it, "the hard work has already been done". More than one interviewee commented that it is now taken for granted that on social action and other issues, Churches will generally work together in a way which in previous decades was not the case. 'Practical ecumenism' or the 'ecumenism of action' is a reality. Many of the interviewees were keen to stress this and therefore emphasise the 'gift' aspect of unity.

However, the corollary of that success is that, in the words of one leader "it has all become familiar" and, accordingly, in the words of another, "it doesn't feel like a priority any more". In fact, the ecumenical officer of one of the larger Churches summarised the whole of ecumenism as needing "a reboot, it's taken for granted and needs a new mission". He lamented that many local areas don't even bother with the Week of Prayer for Christian Unity (an annual international event in which Churches are encouraged to gather together to hold meetings and pray for Christian unity) any more because they don't see the need. Another interviewee stated bluntly that it was "flogging a dead horse if we think that there is any structure that will get a great deal of energy if it is dressed up as ecumenism."

Those Churches and interviewees who were particularly concerned with striving for "visible unity" were among the most disillusioned with the current state of ecumenism. So, one leader of an Orthodox Church summed up the feelings of many of his fellow Orthodox leaders when he said "people have lost hope in the visible unity of the Church", while another, from a mainstream Protestant Church, conceded that he had lost confidence in the possibility of "real unity". Progress, in his words, was "slow and faltering". That being the case, it is perhaps little surprise that they struggled to articulate a mission and purpose for CTE as an instrument for delivering their vision for ecumenism.

However, it was not only among those Churches who emphasise the 'calling' dimension and visibility of unity that this sense of a missing vision was apparent. For one leader of a Charismatic denomination, CTE disappointed because on the big social issues "[it] doesn't seem to be able to nail its colours to the mast". This was a sentiment echoed by a number of Pentecostal and Charismatic leaders, who felt CTE's inability to speak up on particular issues, such as human sexuality, undermined any sense of its purpose. This is linked to what they see CTE as providing for them, to which we shall be return below, and views on liberalism and social issues, which is dealt with in the specific weaknesses section.

Another way in which this thinness of vision came up was in trying to identify the USP (Unique Selling Point) of CTE vis-à-vis other ecumenical bodies. Most of the CTE members were also members of other ecumenical organisations or took part in bilateral processes. What then did CTE provide that Churches could not get from other bodies? Some things were identifiable (see 'strengths' section), but one Pentecostal leader spoke for many across the theological divide when he said that if CTE was to improve or build on what it has now it has to

> *If CTE was to improve or build on what it has now it has to "paint a picture for people… to get the message across" as to what CTE can really do for them that no one else can.*

"paint a picture for people… to get the message across" as to what CTE can really do for them that no one else can.

2   disproportionality in appeal to different Churches

This is tied closely to the issue of purpose or 'Unique Selling Point' discussed above. One ecumenical officer of a larger Church was frank about this: "Coming from a large Church we don't need CTE as much as other Churches". He went on to say that he felt that his particular Church could survive quite happily without CTE. He was keen to stress that this did not mean he saw no value in CTE, but given that his own Church had a significant public voice, and reasonably sized staff they didn't need many of the services CTE provided as much as smaller Churches did.

Another interviewee from the same Church broadly agreed, and noted that the level of importance attached to CTE was disproportionate to the amount of funding provided, which in his Church's case he deemed to be "significant". More broadly he remarked that when you draw up the annual budgets "you always work out what is essential, what is necessary and what is nice, and to be really honest a lot of the ecumenism comes into the nice category."

By contrast, many of the smaller Churches saw CTE as playing a much more significant role. One, for example, saw it as a means for small communities to speak out as "spokesperson for all Christians". A number of the smaller Churches, Pentecostal, Charismatic, Protestant and Orthodox had interviewees who voiced hopes that CTE could own that role in terms of public advocacy.

3   lack of public profile and wish that CTE would speak out more

There is a visibility issue for CTE as an organisation. This is true both internally within the Christian community and in terms of broader public visibility. The leader of one of the larger Churches reckoned that "at least 85% [of that Church's believers] will have never heard of CTE or any other ecumenical body". This was echoed broadly across the board. Some of the members, who are themselves networks of churches, reported a failing on their own part to report on what they did in CTE effectively across their Churches. This, naturally, has consequences for that idea of finding a purpose and strapline. Unless CTE is visible, how can it make a case for itself?

'Presidents of CTE should speak on more issues with one voice'

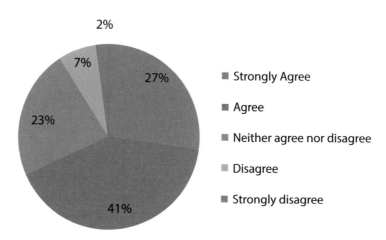

The visibility question is also an issue in terms of broader public visibility. A majority of CTE members want to see the presidents of CTE speaking out on more issues with one voice: 68% of respondents to the survey at the Enabling Group agreed or strongly agreed on this, while only 7% disagreed. However, many interviewees conceded that while that was fine in principle, in practice it was difficult for CTE to get its message out there. "Journalists know who the Cardinal is and who the Archbishop of Canterbury is, they don't know who CTE is" said one Church leader. This lack of public profile is a weakness if CTE is meant to be speaking out on issues that matter to members.

> There is a visibility issue for CTE as an organisation. This is true both internally within the Christian community and in terms of broader public visibility.

It also ties into a related issue, which is that there is demand for CTE, and the presidents in particular, to be a more prominent Christian voice, and a sense among many interviewees that opportunities are being missed in this regard. This was particularly true among Pentecostal and Charismatic interviewees. One, for example, expressed his disappointment with the presidents, saying that he felt "maybe I set expectations too high, but I thought it could be more… I thought they'd be able to really speak to the spiritual welfare of the nation".

Part of the issue here is that, in line with point two above, some of the Churches need that public advocacy more than others. Another is that the members are not in agreement about what the issues are that the presidents should speak out on. Our interviewees most commonly wanted to see the presidents speak out in response to terrorist attacks and about Christian persecution (particularly abroad). Beyond those there was far less consensus, with suggestions ranging from gay marriage, to political issues, to statements seeking Christian unity, to recognition and lobbying on particular international issues (the Armenian Christian, communities in Africa and the Middle East for various others).

4 finance

Most interviewees who felt they understood the CTE financial position had concerns about its sustainability. Interviewees from member Churches were asked what it would take for them to increase their financial support. A number of the smaller Churches and the historic Protestant Churches confessed to being under significant financial strain and gave no indication they were in a position to increase contributions. Several interviewees from smaller Churches admitted, in fact, to being more focused simply on survival.

A second set of responses did not rule out an increase in financial support but wanted much more clarity about what that would get them. This again ties back into the need for a clearer vision as outlined above. One general secretary noted that "if increased funding was requested we'd need to understand what we're getting that we couldn't get on our own". Another, from one of the historic Protestant Churches noted the need to "prove what it is for" and to have "something to show for it", and suggested that projects might be easier to fund than structures.

Some of the Churches, particularly from the Pentecostal and Charismatic constituency but also some among the Orthodox, saw the responsibility for funding as lying primarily, or even solely, with the Church of England (and some of the other larger Churches), with one going so far as to call it their "moral responsibility".

This suggestion was, perhaps unsurprisingly, not welcomed by the larger Churches. For one thing, tying in with the point above, some from the largest Churches felt that they got the least out of CTE and that, therefore, it would be hard to justify increasing their support. More than one interviewee from larger Churches said that the system at present was not right and that some of the other Churches ought to be expected to pay their way. One interviewee from the Church of England protested against the implication that their support was in doubt, pointing to the fact that they remain the largest financial supporter and also commit significant working hours to CTE.

One suggestion that came from several sources was to cease relying on member subscriptions and seek outside funding, particularly for more projects. The situation may also be alleviated if a stronger vision could be articulated for the organisation as a whole. Either way, this is clearly an ongoing tension between different constituencies within CTE and one that looks difficult to overcome.

5   lack of nimbleness

Related to the issue of structures above is the criticism that CTE lacks "nimbleness". One Orthodox leader, for example, described CTE as often being "slow" and having "sleepy machinery". He suggested that part of the issue was that too many Churches didn't like to be spoken for and so it took a long time to canvas and agree a direction for any statements or decisions.

Many of the smaller and newer Churches in particular were frustrated at this slowness. Since those Churches tend to have less organisational structure, they were used to being able to take decisions quickly and get on with doing things. This raised something of a cultural clash with those larger Churches for whom decision making tends to run through more complex structural processes. One interviewee from a larger Church, for example, was wary of CTE making more statements and public pronouncements, because the departments of their Church that were responsible for public affairs were different from those responsible for ecumenism, and they didn't want to cause confusion or provoke territorial conflicts.

An inability to respond quickly was also a criticism from some outsiders. One interviewee, who was not part of CTE but had long experience of ecumenism and had worked with CTE on a project in the past, recorded his frustration with a missed opportunity in the past. CTE had partnered with him to try and provide opportunities to a younger generation of ecumenists and sent a group to the World Youth Day celebrations.

The interviewee's frustrations were, first, that he had found it extremely difficult to use CTE to get the word out. Messages were meant to be sent out by member Churches to the grassroots, but it seemed like that often didn't happen, and there was a breakdown in communications. Second, he had hoped to be able to build on this opportunity and stay in touch with the young people and raise them up as an asset for the future. Things took too long to organise and the moment was lost. For the interviewee that was the key weakness of CTE: it was a bit cumbersome and found it difficult to link projects to the grassroots.

Which of the following comes closest to describing your view of the future of ecumenism in the UK?

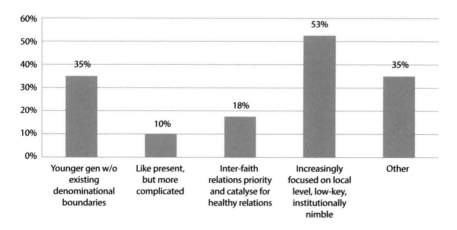

It is worth noting that there is demand among CTE members for change in this regard. In the survey circulated by Theos to the CTE Enabling Group, one question focused on the future of CTE, with the most popular available answer being: "Ecumenism will be increasingly focused on the local level, low-key in its tone and approach, and institutionally nimble".

6   Intermediate Bodies (IBs)

Intermediate Bodies (IBs) are networks for ecumenical partnerships organised at regional or county level. They are a unique feature of Church life in England, found nowhere else in the world, and were originally set up to care for and oversee local ecumenical partnerships (LEPs) and to "support and encourage local unity".[1] The category of Intermediate Bodies was formalised as a result of the 1987 three-nations Swanwick conference on ecumenism, which also marked the birth of national ecumenical instruments.

Intermediate Bodies, such as Birmingham Churches Together or Churches Together in Cumbria, are independent of CTE as an organisation, and often function as informal networks of Churches in a particular county or (metropolitan) area who have shared goals and coordinate on joint initiatives.

The interviews we conducted revealed there is some confusion as to how IBs work, what role they serve, how they fit into the larger ecology of English ecumenism and, more specifically, what is their precise relationship to CTE as an organisation. Some interviewees expressed concern that many IBs had folded and that the picture of intermediate ecumenism in the country was quite patchy despite CTE's declared aim to resource and support IBs.[2] A number of interviewees expressed a desire for CTE to increase its efforts in resourcing IBs, by connecting up and mapping ecumenical initiatives.

> *CTE should be more intentional about tapping into areas where there is a vibrant local ecumenism.*

In terms of strategy, it was suggested that CTE should be more intentional about tapping into areas where there is a vibrant local ecumenism; harvest information such as examples of best practice, success stories etc.; disseminate these widely; and consider recruiting regional ecumenical leaders, preferably from the younger generation, that have the backing and validation of the communities in which they are active.

7   lack of appeal to the next generation

Following on from the point above, a number of interviewees, representing a range across denominational lines, saw the lack of a younger generation involved in ecumenism as a reason for concern. One interviewee, while being briefed on the project and the sorts of person who had been interviewed so far immediately asked "and how many of them have been under 50?". The honest answer was "very few". Of course, on one level this is unsurprising, the majority of the interviews were conducted with senior leaders within the Churches. However, engaging younger people in ecumenism, particularly within the structures of a body like CTE was proving difficult. More than one interviewee felt this was a problem across the ecumenical scene. One, for example, said of local ecumenism that it was often characterised by "people with views 50 years out of date who think it is cutting edge to talk to other Christians". Another lamented the fact that there were so few roles available for younger people, going so far as to propose the need for a CTE "youth president".

It is worth noting that this failure to engage younger people was not usually blamed on CTE, but more on the Churches themselves. England's Christian community is itself ageing and finding roles for younger people is a challenge that goes far beyond the ecumenical scene. It is also worth saying that this once again links back to the need for a vision. Older ecumenists are there because they've been working on these issues for a long time. If there was a clearer vision or purpose it would perhaps be easier to raise a new generation to push that vision forwards.

> A clearer alignment of ecumenical efforts with mission and witness may be a significant step towards addressing some of the current challenges of ecumenism.

The final section of this report will, in fact, suggest that a clearer alignment of ecumenical efforts with mission and witness – two of the most frequently mentioned focal points for the future of ecumenism – may be a significant step towards addressing some of the current challenges of ecumenism, including youth participation, in England.

Engaging and involving the younger generation would mean not only ensuring that ecumenical work is carried out into the future and the legacy of previous generations' hard work is not wasted, but would likely bring fresh energy. On a practical level, younger ecumenical workers may be better suited to help with developing digital and social media capacity, reflecting the fact that a number of interviewees saw the need for ecumenism to take advantage of the advances in technology and particularly the social media revolution.

8 church decline

The general decline in the numbers of people regularly attending church is not, of course, a weakness of CTE's making, but it has direct consequences for CTE as an organisation. It is related to the issues of finance and of the next generation as highlighted above. Simply put, Christianity on the whole is declining across the country. In the 2001 census, 72% of people in England and Wales called themselves Christian. In 2011, that had reduced to 59%. The latest British Social Attitudes Survey claims that just short of 50% of people in Britain now consider themselves to have "no religion".[3]

The consequences of this are being felt in a number of CTE's member Churches, with several feeling under severe strain. Some of the smaller Churches were, in their own words, "fighting just to survive". Some felt betrayed by the other Churches who had failed to help with spaces for worship or support when they needed it.

Some of the historic Protestant Churches reported a severe shortage of volunteers to do ecumenical work. One admitted that they are not attending as many meetings as they would like within CTE because they simply lack the people to attend. This is a weakness more of the members than CTE itself, but it poses an existential question to CTE in terms of how it adapts to this new situation.

specific weaknesses and areas of concern

The weaknesses outlined above were reported across a broad cross-section of CTE members, representing different theological constituencies.

Aside from those broadly shared concerns, there were also a number of weaknesses which were specific in the sense that they tended to come only from one particular constituency or group of churches (e.g. historic Protestant, Orthodox, Pentecostal, Charismatic, or as defined by size). The fact that these are not as widely identified as weaknesses does not make them less important. Indeed, unless some of them can be addressed they will, in turn, undermine efforts at defining a common vision or rectifying the financial issues, since if a particular group becomes disillusioned with CTE on account of these weaknesses, that may prevent the organisation as a whole from making progress.

These specific issues have been grouped under these six headings:

1   Ecclesiologies: "for there are many"

2   Should CTE focus on inter-faith relations?

3   A lack of ambition to seek visible unity

4   The particular status of black and ethnic minority Churches

5   Conflicting social views

6   Relationship to CTBI

1   ecclesiologies: "for there are many"

This is a grouping together of a number of related concerns. Some of them are practical challenges raised by particular Churches. For example, there is a basic issue about territorial boundaries and ecclesiology. CTE is a national organisation for England, but a number of its members do not divide themselves along such national grounds. The Catholic Church has a Bishops' Conference for England and Wales, and of course is part of an international Church whose doctrine is managed from Rome.

Several of the Orthodox leaders were responsible for the whole of the British Isles and again, sit in international structures. At the other end of the spectrum, there are a number of Pentecostal and Charismatic Churches that are effectively, in the words of one interviewee, "mega house churches", and do not fit a national model for rather different reasons.

The challenge goes beyond territorial boundaries to ecclesiology. It will always be difficult to deliver a unified vision and to speak out on issues of common concern when you have some Churches (e.g. the Baptist Union of Great Britain, the Congregational Federation) with a highly decentralised ecclesiology alongside other Churches with more centralised structures. On the one hand, Churches with hierarchical ecclesiologies and centralised structures are split between those that require cross-departmental consultations and those that are able to respond immediately. On the other hand, many of the representatives from Churches with decentralised ecclesiologies (who now make up a significant part of CTE membership), were keen to stress the diversity among

> *The challenge is to shape a vision that allows for the inclusion and full participation of Churches with decentralised ecclesiologies and an ingrained 'grassroots ethos', alongside Churches which operate on the basis of a more hierarchical model.*

and within their own Churches. This led to difficulties, (even, sometimes, impossibilities), of representing a unified viewpoint or implementing a particular vision during official consultations within CTE. The challenge is, therefore, to shape a vision that allows for the inclusion and full participation of Churches with decentralised ecclesiologies and an ingrained 'grassroots ethos', alongside Churches which operate on the basis of a more hierarchical model.

Some of the consequences of this diversity can also be seen in specific concerns raised over particular issues of doctrine and theology. For example, several Orthodox and Catholic interviewees were concerned that particular aspects of worship or theological discussion were conducted in a distinctively Protestant way during CTE meetings, with one interviewee noting that he still felt there were "some subtle anti-Catholic slurs". This view was not necessarily widely shared even among Orthodox and Catholic interviewees, but did come up more prominently when discussion turned to either joint worship or joint Bible study. One Pentecostal interviewee noted that that had been more of an issue historically, with a challenge in the 1990s among Pentecostals who viewed Catholics as "outside their willing reach".

2   should CTE focus on inter-faith relations?

The vast majority of interviewees felt that there was something important about ecumenism and doing things as Christians, as opposed to simply doing multi-faith work. However, a few interviewees, particularly those from liberal Protestant Churches did seem to have an interest in broadening things out to a more inter-faith outlook. This is borne out in the survey results, with 7% of respondents answering that the function of CTE was "to promote inter-faith dialogue", and 34% agreeing that CTE "should do more in the area of inter-faith relations" (though 48% disagreed with that statement).

This is not a majority view, but it is a significant enough minority to be worth further discussion as CTE looks at its future activities.

'CTE should do more in the area of inter-faith relations'

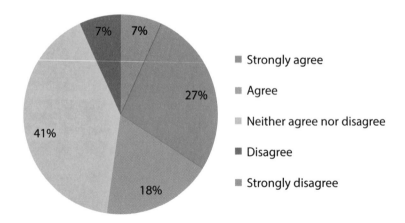

3   a lack of vision to seek visible unity

"People have lost hope in the visible unity of the Church," remarked one Orthodox interviewee. It was a sentiment echoed by a group of interviewees who clove to a vision of visible Christian unity and stressed the 'calling' dimension of unity more than its 'gift' aspect. This view, it must be stressed, was not a majority opinion among interviewees but was frequently heard among Orthodox and Catholic interviewees and also among a set of interviewees who believed that the experiments of the 1970s had never gone far enough.

So, for example, one interviewee who had had a long association with CTE and its predecessor bodies felt that "the problem with ecumenism is that it's been written off without ever really being tried". A group of interviewees felt strongly that there was a real need for more theological discussion. One, for example, argued that CTE has "lost its way on doctrine" and needs to "talk solid stuff" such as Baptism and the Eucharist. One leader of an Orthodox Church said that they felt that ecumenism had "taken the easy way out… just focusing on social issues". The accusation that, theologically, ecumenism has now reached "lowest common denominator" status was shared by a small, but convinced subset of interviewees.

Against that group, as noted earlier in the report, was a much larger group who didn't want to get back into those issues and mode of ecumenism, believing the points of difference in doctrine and praxis to be either unsolvable or simply too difficult to tackle head on. One historic Protestant Church felt that they already had to sign too many ecumenical agreements that they didn't really agree with theologically. Given their theology and ecclesiology, they confessed to being unable to sign up to some of the statements, which resulted in the feeling that they were outsiders to the process. Another historic Protestant Church interviewee was frank in admitting that whatever else they would miss if CTE were to close "we wouldn't miss the theological stuff". According to our survey, only 9% felt the primary function of CTE was "Theological training and resourcing".

4   the particular status of black and ethnic minority Churches

It is important to caveat what follows with the fact that the diversity of CTE and range of its membership is considered one of its greatest strengths. Having a CTE President drawn from the Pentecostal Churches was taken by a number of members to be a sign of positive progress, and the efforts of CTE staff to engage with black Churches in particular received a great deal of praise.

However, there was still a sense in which the integration of, on the one hand, black Pentecostal Churches and, on the other, Orthodox Churches remained a challenge. While all representatives from this segment of CTE members recognise and are grateful for CTE's active efforts at inclusion, many of the ones we spoke to suggested more work is needed to ensure healthy relationships are cultivated and maintained across cultural and ethnic distinctions.

Several interviewees reported there was still a sense in which CTE was "a white man's show" in which the Pentecostal Churches were the poor relations. One interviewee felt this issue was, to an extent, self-inflicted, with too few champions having been raised from within the tradition. In the light of this, some interviewees were keen to suggest that a permanent role for multicultural relations be kept within CTE to secure progress hitherto made and to continue building toward full reconciliation. Many of the representatives from black Churches expressed a heartfelt desire to be self-consciously treated as brothers and sisters in Christ, in "covenantal not contractual terms", as one representative put it, and for all sense of "suspicion" towards them to disappear.

Some interviewees made reference to the old Racial Justice Commission, which they felt still had more work to do. The Commission, it must be noted, was never a CTE project, but had been passed on from the old British Council of Churches to its successor body, Churches Together in Britain in Ireland (CTBI). When CTBI was forced to drastically downsize (from over 50 staff to five), the Commission turned into a Network, and was eventually discontinued.

At the other end of the spectrum, several Orthodox interviewees reported a growing sense of distance from the way in which CTE organised collective worship during the Enabling Group and Forum meetings. More than one reported feeling isolated by a style of worship that seemed alien to them, and felt that the particular concerns of their tradition were ignored or side-lined versus, in the words of one, "a distinctively Protestant style".

> "Increasingly it's social issues which are more of a barrier than the theological."

This is a weakness which can be overstated. Most interviewees felt that the diversity of CTE was a great strength and that strides had been made in terms of integration. However, a significant group of interviewees across a spectrum of traditions did highlight this issue of integration as an area of ongoing concern and something to be monitored in the future.

5 conflicting social views

In the words of one Protestant leader there is an ongoing issue, which is that "there is no common mind" between liberal and theologically conservative Churches. Gay marriage, and to a lesser extent women in leadership positions, remain divisive issues between Churches. One Orthodox leader said that "increasingly it's social issues which are more of a barrier than the theological". Another went further still, saying that when it came to homosexuality "it's sin and we'll never move on that".

A Catholic interviewee said that "in some ways we're further from unity than we were twenty years ago" and some things, such as women priests and gay marriage, "now seem insurmountable". One smaller Protestant Church said that the issues of homosexuality and women priests were the "two big unaddressed issues" in CTE and if they were ever to be defined at an institutional level in a way their Church deemed unacceptable they would be forced to leave. That was a view endorsed by the leader of a Pentecostal Church – in the event that CTE defined its position on particular social issues they would be forced to reconsider their membership. This, according to another interviewee, had been a concern for some Pentecostal Churches before joining; they did not wish to be painted as "liberal by association". On the other side of the argument, interviewees from some of the liberal Protestant Churches had felt, in the words of one interviewee "quite bruised for taking some of our stances." They felt that there had been some "nasty encounters".

It would be an exaggeration to say that this was a big concern for all, or even necessarily the majority of Catholic, Orthodox and Pentecostal interviewees, and many had reconciled themselves to differences on these issues just as they had on worship, scripture and sacraments. Nonetheless the issue was named as a concern by a significant minority of interviewees.

6   relationship to CTBI

An overwhelming number of those interviewed found the relationship between CTE and CTBI (Churches Together in Britain and Ireland) unclear. Fifty-nine per cent of those we surveyed 'agreed' and 27% 'strongly agreed' with the statement "We would like more clarity on the relationship between and respective functions of CTE and CTBI". One respondent inquired: "Do we need CTE and CTBI? If so, why? Keep structures simple to

'We would like more clarity on the relationship and respective functions of CTE to CTBI'

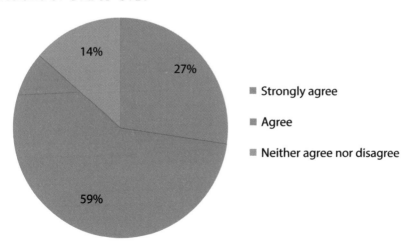

14%

27%

59%

■ Strongly agree

■ Agree

■ Neither agree nor disagree

serve real needs!" Other respondents raised concerns about the risk of duplication and overlap between the two.

Interviewees who were more familiar with the history of ecumenism in England suggested that the covenant which brought CTE and CTBI into existence needs to be renegotiated. "CTBI as successor to British Council of Churches received assets and resources but CTE is virtually without assets. This is a huge mistake," said one such interviewee.

Like many of the weaknesses and areas of concern discussed above, the relationship between CTE and CTBI would also be helped if CTE succeeded in articulating a clearer vision and specific focus.

chapter 3 – references

1   http://www.cte.org.uk/Groups/234725/Home/About/County_Intermediate_Bodies/County_Intermediate_Bodies.aspx. Site accessed 24 July 2017.

2   Ibid.

3   http://bsa.natcen.ac.uk/latest-report/british-social-attitudes-28/religion.aspx. Site accessed 2 August 2017.

4

possibilities for the future and recommendations

1   continue cultivating relationships

In the first section of this report we noted that while Christianity in England has generally been declining in numbers it has become increasingly diverse in its expressions. CTE has made efforts to reflect the huge variety of Christian life in England in the structure of its membership. This is seen by most interviewees as a positive development. Key to this end has been CTE's much appreciated role in brokering and cultivating relationships between Churches. Indeed, as previously noted, relationship-building was one of the most valued functions of CTE. CTE members clearly want the organisation to continue acting as a relational catalyst for ecumenical work in England, whatever the precise focus of this work might be in the future (more on this below).

As a practical way of continuing to strengthen relationships between its members, CTE may consider drawing on an approach taken by the National Council of Churches USA during the years it was led by Michael Kinnamon.[1] Briefly, the Council decided to organise visits to each of the member Churches of the Council. Rather than having only NCC staff on the delegation, they invited representatives from other member Churches to come along. The visits would unfold after the same pattern. The team of visitors would worship with their hosts in the style of the host Church, share a meal, exchange gifts and engage in conversation around the following questions:

- When we (the other members) pray for you (the Church being visited), for what should we pray?

- What gifts has God entrusted to you that you hope to offer within the fellowship of the council?

- What gifts do you need/hope to receive?

- What are the biggest challenges you are likely to face in the years ahead?

- What do you intend to do to strengthen your relationship with other members?[2]

After the visits, the delegation would write the host a summary of the discussion. It was often the case that the letter received would be circulated among the parishes or local churches of the host member. This, writes Kinnamon, was both an expression of and a means to deeper mutual commitment.[3]

This practical approach is something that the leadership of CTE may wish to consider as it seeks to continue playing its most valued role, namely, brokering and fostering relationships. While the importance of relationships was acknowledged across the board, however, a large number of interviewees, as previously noted, wanted greater clarity on the vision underpinning CTE's laudable efforts at relationship-building. Further thoughts and recommendations on this point are offered below.

2 clarify vision

In light of the previous sections, on CTE's strengths, weaknesses and areas of concern, we recommend CTE considers clarifying and sharpening its vision: why does it exist? What does it do uniquely? Or as one interviewee put it "Churches Together in England for... what?" It should have become apparent that most of the challenges faced by CTE and weaknesses perceived by

> We recommend CTE considers clarifying and sharpening its vision: why does it exist? What does it do uniquely?

members would be at least partly resolved by arriving at and adhering to a clearer vision. As an example we refer to CTE's relationship to CTBI, which an overwhelming majority of those interviewed found unclear. Fifty-nine per cent of those we surveyed 'agreed' and 27% 'strongly agreed' with the statement "We would like more clarity on the relationship between and respective functions of CTE and CTBI". No one disagreed.

The need for a clearer vision and purpose is apparent, yet the challenge of addressing this issue is, of course, significant, particularly given CTE's breadth and its members' diverse theologies, ecclesiologies and ethical stances. There are however possibilities to be explored.

3 consider a clearer focus on mission

We previously noted that the category of mission framed a large number of interviewees' responses to our request for ecumenical 'success stories' and suggestions for moving forward into the future. While recognising that mission is a fundamental dimension and concern of ecumenism in general, and indeed of CTE, our research revealed a growing desire for a firmer alignment of English ecumenism with mission. A significant number of

Mission framed a large number of interviewees' responses to our request for ecumenical 'success stories' and suggestions for moving forward into the future. Our research revealed a growing desire for a firmer alignment of English ecumenism with mission.

people we spoke to wanted to see CTE more intentionally geared towards mission and witness.

Based on the suggestions offered during the interviews, it is clear that member Churches conceive of mission in terms not only of evangelisation – although there was wide agreement that this is a priority, particularly in a climate of Church decline – but also of social action, peace-making and reconciliation, other aspects of social justice, and creation care. Of course, not all Churches pursue all of the above areas of Christian mission and witness with equal vigour and emphasis. Open conversations would hopefully bring out areas of agreement and lead to an increase in partnerships. In connection with this, one of the most frequent recommendations we heard during interviews was that CTE should consider increasing its role in facilitating partnerships on mission at all levels and become an informing and facilitating body for mission-focused ecumenical work in England.

CTE, suggested some interviewees, should seek to become the 'go to' place for resources and information on all missional initiatives and partnerships across the country. It should be more intentional and technologically savvy in disseminating this information as widely as possible, harnessing the power of new technologies and particularly social media. CTE has nothing to lose from connecting with and inviting young people into a mission-focused ecumenical life. We therefore take note of and applaud the emphasis on youth participation at the 2018 Forum.

There is a danger, however, that beneath such familiar terms such as mission and witness lie deep differences. CTE should therefore consider hosting and facilitating substantive conversations with its members about the nature, scope and practicalities of mission to discern what reshaping ecumenical work around mission would look like in practice. This is important given the high likelihood that a missional mode of relating would eventually throw up the old, unsolved ecumenical problems (e.g. the recognition of ministry and the reconciliation of episcopal and non-episcopal ministries), particularly if mission is undertaken in a territorial way. The recommendation is therefore to take mission seriously, but remain alert and prepared to engage the differences as and when they resurface.

4 the public value of ecumenism

Several interviewees, when asked to envision ecumenical life five or ten years into the future, spoke about the important contribution ecumenism could make to public life. In an age of deep diversity, polarisation, and large scale global migration, something of the ethos, disciplines, successes and struggles of ecumenism could be offered as a gift to the broader society. Living with deep differences, welcoming the stranger, and the ongoing challenge of keeping unity in rich diversity are just a few areas where ecumenism can be offered as a form of political gift. This is a suggestion which several interviewees either explicitly made or intimated.

The practicalities of this would have to be, of course, discussed in detail and agreed upon within CTE's decision-making forums. While the presidents seem best placed to act on this suggestion, CTE may consider exploring ways of implementing it at other levels of ecumenical life.

5 speak with one voice

In closing, we return to CTE members' appetite for 'speaking with one voice' through the office of the presidents. As noted earlier, 68% of respondents to our survey agreed or strongly agreed that presidents should speak with one voice on more issues. Given CTE's breadth, the main challenge this raises is reaching agreement on the issues presidents might speak on. There is no easy way of overcoming this challenge, of course, but clarifying one's strategic vision and primary focus is surely an important step to this end. It is conceivable that a clearer vision, owned by all CTE members, focused on mission and the Church's vocation in the world, would help bring out agreed issues on which CTE might speak into the public square.

chapter 4 – references

1   The largest ecumenical body in the United States, established in 1950, which currently has 38 member Churches.

2   Michael Kinnamon, *Can a Renewal Movement Be Renewed?: Questions for the Future of Ecumenism* (Grand Rapids, MI / Cambridge, UK: Wm. B. Eerdmans, 2014), p. 12.

3   Ibid.

appendix

Interviews conducted with representatives of CTE member Churches and networks:

	Church / Network	Persons interviewed:
1	Antiochian Orthodox Church	George Hackney
2	Apostolic Pastoral Congress	Doye Agama
3	Armenian Orthodox Church	Hovakim Manukyan
4	Baptist Union of Great Britain	Lynn Green, Hilary Treavis, Stephen Keyworth
5	Catholic Bishops' Conference of England and Wales	Chris Thomas, Robert Byrne, Bernard Longley, Vincent Nichols
6	Church of England	William Nye, Roger Paul, Jeremy Worthen, William Adam
7	Church of Scotland (Presbytery of England)	John McPake
8	Churches in Communities International	Trevor Howard, Hugh Osgood
9	Congregational Federation	Yvonne Campbell, Janet Wootton, Judith Mbaabu, Phil Wood, Kathryn Young, Barry Osborne
10	Coptic Orthodox Church	Anba Angaelos
11	Council of African & Caribbean Churches UK	Olu Abiola
12	Council of Lutheran Churches	James Laing
13	Elim Pentecostal Church	Chris Cartwright, Stephen Fowler
14	Evangelical Lutheran Church of England	John Ehlers
15	Evangelische Synode Deutscher Sprache in Großbritannien	Albrecht Köstlin-Büürma, Oliver Fischer

16	Free Church of England	John Fenwick
17	Free Churches Group	Hugh Osgood, Paul Rochester
18	Ichthus Christian Fellowship	Roger Foster, David Curtis
19	Independent Methodist Church	Brian Rowney & Bill Hampson
20	International Ministerial Council of Great Britain	Sheila Douglas
21	Ixthus Church Council	Costakis Evangelou
22	Joint Council for Anglo-Caribbean Churches	Creswell Green
23	Malankara Orthodox Syrian Church	Elizabeth Joy, Zachariah Mar Nicholovos
24	Mar Thoma Church	Zac Varghese
25	Methodist Church	Gareth Powell, Neil Stubbens
26	Moravian Church	Philip Cooper, Zoe Ferdinand, Bob Hopcroft, Gillian Taylor
27	New Testament Assembly	Delroy Powell
28	Oecumenical Patriarchate	Gillian Crow
29	Pioneer	Billy Kennedy
30	Redeemed Christian Church of God	Agu Irukwu
31	Religious Society of Friends	Paul Parker, Marigold Bentley, Helen Griffith
32	Russian Orthodox Church	Stephen Platt
33	Salvation Army	Jonathan Roberts, Clive Adams
34	Transatlantic and Pacific Alliance of Churches	Paul Hackman
35	Unification Council of Cherubim & Seraphim Churches	John Adegoke
36	United Kingdom World Evangelism Trust	Simon Iheanacho
37	United Reformed Church	John Proctor, David Tatem, John Ellis
38	Wesleyan Holiness Church	Clement Bartlett

All other interviews conducted for this research:

	Name	Organisation / Role
39	Bob Fyfe	General Secretary of Churches Together in Britain and Ireland
40	Callan Slipper	Focolare Movement
41	Christopher Foster	Bishop of Portsmouth, CTE Director
42	Colin Marsh	Ecumenical Development Officer, Birmingham
43	David Thompson	Emeritus Professor of Modern Church History, University of Cambridge, and Chairman of CTE's Theology and Unity Group
44	Donald Allister	Bishop of Peterborough, Chair of the Church of England's Council for Christian Unity
45	Eric Brown	CTE President
46	Jenny Bond	CTE, Training, Resourcing and Evets
47	Jim Currin	CTE, Evangelisation, Mission and Media
48	Joe Aldred	CTE, Pentecostal and Multicultural Relations
49	Mark Woodruff	Sainsbury Family Trust
50	Roger Sutton	'Gather' Network
51	Ruth Bottoms	CTE, Vice-Chair of Board
52	Ruth Gee	CTE, Deputy Moderator of the CTE Forum
53	Tim Watson	Chemin Neuf
54	Vincent Nichols	Cardinal Archbishop of Westminster, President of CTE

Disclaimer:

A few representatives of CTE members could not be interviewed for this project. They were either unavailable or could not be reached during the period in which this research was carried out.